LLC vs. S-Corp vs. C-Corp

Explained in 100 Pages or Less

Disclaimer

This book is not intended to be a substitute for personalized advice from a professional accountant or attorney. Nothing contained within this text should be construed as tax advice. The publisher and author make no representation or warranty as to this book's adequacy or appropriateness for any purpose. Similarly, no representation or warranty is made as to the accuracy of the material in this book.

Purchasing this book does not create any client relationship or other advisory, fiduciary, or professional services relationship with the publisher or with the author. *You alone* bear the *sole* responsibility of assessing the merits and risks associated with any financial decisions you make. And it should always be kept in mind that any investment can result in partial or complete loss.

LLC vs. S-Corp vs. C-Corp

Explained in 100 Pages or Less

Mike Piper, CPA

Why is there a light bulb on the cover?

In cartoons and comics, a light bulb is often used to signify a moment of clarity or sudden understanding—an "aha!" moment. My hope is that the books in the ...*in 100 pages or less* series can help readers achieve clarity and understanding of topics that are often considered complex and confusing—hence the light bulb.

Dedication

For you, the reader, as you create a
business that you can be proud of.

Your Feedback is Appreciated!

As the author of this book, I'm very interested to hear your thoughts. If you find the book helpful, please let me know. Alternatively, if you have any suggestions of ways to make the book better, I'm eager to hear that, too.

Finally, if you're dissatisfied with your purchase for any reason, let me know, and I'll be happy to provide you with a refund of the current list price of the book (limited to one refund per title per household).

You can reach me at: mike@simplesubjects.com.

Best Regards,
Mike Piper, CPA

Table of Contents

Part Two
LLC, C-Corp, or S-Corp

Introduction

Like the other books in the *...in 100 Pages or Less* series, this book seeks to offer an easy-to-understand explanation of a rather technical topic.

But plenty of books do that.

What makes the books in this series unique is that they seek to offer their explanations in as concise a manner as possible. With this book, the assumption is that you want to determine which type of legal entity is best for your business, and that—after making that decision—you want to go back to running the business that you love (rather than reading another 300 pages about limited liability companies, S-corporations, and C-corporations).

Why the Question of Entity Selection is So Crucial

How you structure your business is going to affect a myriad of things from how much tax you'll have to pay on your profits, to how your business will be treated in a lawsuit, to what type of checking account your bank will let you open.

Make the right decision, and you'll be paying less tax, you'll know your personal assets are protected from lawsuits against your business, and you might even save yourself some money on accounting costs.

Make the wrong decision, and you'll be paying an unnecessary amount of tax, and you could be just a lawsuit away from losing your home and other personal assets.

The Goal of This Book

The purpose of this guide is to give you a basic understanding of the advantages and disadvantages of the various legal structures for a business. The goal is *not* to make you an expert on any of the tax or legal matters discussed.

Quite in fact, after reading this book, it still might be a wise decision to meet with an accountant and/or an attorney to get some personalized advice.

So why bother reading the book at all? My hopes are as follows:

a) Some business owners will realize that, at least for them, the decision isn't *too* complicated, and
b) Those of you who decide it would still be wise to visit with a professional will at least have a basic level of understanding ahead of time.

Having a ground-level understanding before meeting with a pro will both cut your meeting shorter (thereby saving you money) and help you to better understand the advice you receive.

A Brief Outline

This book is broken down into two main sections:

1) A discussion of the pros and cons of the default legal structures (sole proprietorships and partnerships), as it's most likely that your business is currently operating as one of the two, and

2) An analysis of the advantages gained by forming an LLC, S-corp, or C-corp, as well as what you stand to lose by forming any of the above.

PART ONE

Sole Proprietorships and Partnerships

CHAPTER ONE

Sole Proprietorships: An Overview

All you have to do to form a sole proprietorship is start doing business. (At least, that's all the federal government requires you to do.) That is, any business started by a single person is automatically a sole proprietorship unless the owner decides to take some action (such as incorporating) in order to become a different type of entity.

Local Requirements for Starting a Sole Proprietorship

It's likely that your state, county, or city has somewhat more time-consuming (and money-consuming) requirements for forming a sole proprietorship than the federal government does.

Depending upon what type of business you want to start (e.g., a restaurant, a freelance writing business, etc.), your city may require you to get a license of one sort or another, and that license will often be accompanied by a licensing fee. Fortunately, the local fees for starting a business are usually modest.

Taxpayer IDs

An Employer Identification Number (EIN)—also referred to as a taxpayer ID—is to a business what a Social Security number is to an individual. It gives the federal government a way to keep track of you.

As we'll soon discuss, for federal income tax purposes, your sole proprietorship is not a distinct entity from yourself. As a result, unless you have employees or a qualified retirement plan such as a 401(k) for your business, you do not need to get an EIN. However, even if you're not required to get a taxpayer ID for your business, it may be a good idea to do so.

Why? Because, depending upon the nature of your business and who your clients or vendors are, you may have to fill out various forms that require you to provide either your EIN or your Social Security number. Of course, in this age of identity theft, making your Social Security number public information isn't exactly a great idea.

Getting a tax ID is absolutely free, and the entire process only takes a few minutes. Simply visit irs.gov, search for "EIN," and fill out the online application.

State and County Requirements: Will You Need a DBA?

If you plan to do business under a name other than your own, your county or state will probably require you to file a "doing business as" (DBA) statement—sometimes referred to as a "fictitious name" or "assumed name" filing. They may even require you to publish it in a local newspaper. (There are plenty of services that can handle this for you for a reasonable fee.)

The reason for requiring a DBA is that states want to have a name on file for somebody who can be held accountable if a sole proprietorship breaks a law or does something that would result in a civil lawsuit.

EXAMPLE: You have a new porch built by a local construction company named Decadent Decks. The porch ends up looking great, and everything appears to be fine. But then, just one week after the porch is built, it collapses while you're on it, and you break two ribs and a wrist from the fall.

You'll likely want to sue Decadent Decks for (at least) the cost of the medical bills. The only problem is that Decadent Decks is a sole proprietorship. (More on this later, but that basically means that it isn't a legal entity and therefore cannot be sued.) And there is no way to tell from the name of the business who the owner is. Thankfully, your state required the owner of Decadent Decks to file a DBA, so they have his name on record. As a result, you'll be able to sue the owner directly.

Depending upon your state or county's rules, you may not be required to file a DBA if you use your own name within the name of the business. However, other states will require you to get a DBA if your business is named anything other than your exact legal name. For instance, some states would even require a DBA for a Chris Dowdes to start a business called Catering by Chris Dowdes.

Chapter 1 Simple Summary

- Any single-owner business will be a sole proprietorship unless the owner takes an explicit action (such as incorporating) to make it otherwise.

- The federal government doesn't require you to file any documents to form your sole proprietorship.

- Depending on what type of business you plan to operate, your city may require a business license to start a sole proprietorship.

- Many states and counties require you to file a "doing business as" (DBA) statement if you plan to use a name for your business that is not the same as your legal name.

CHAPTER TWO

Sole Proprietorships: Taxation

For the most part, handling the taxes for a sole proprietorship is fairly simple. It comes down to filling out just a few forms.[1]

"Pass-Through" Taxation

Sole proprietorships are known as "pass-through" entities. What this means is that the profit (or loss) from the business is "passed through" to the owner of the business. Therefore, if you run a sole proprietorship, the profit from the business will show up on your regular individual tax return (Form 1040).

---

[1] All federal tax forms are available for download at irs.gov/forms-instructions or via a quick Google search.

Schedule C

Schedule C is where you will compute the profit or loss from your business. Schedule C is little more than a list of all your revenues followed by a list of all your expenses. The end-result of Schedule C is a figure known as your "Net Profit or Loss," which will be carried over to your Form 1040 and taxed at the regular individual income tax rates (as per the following tables).

Single (2020)

Taxable income[1]:	The tax is:
$0 - $9,875	10% of the amount over $0
$9,875 - $40,125	$987.50 plus 12% of the amount over $9,875
$40,125 - $85,525	$4,617.50 plus 22% of the amount over $40,125
$85,525 - $163,300	$14,605.50 plus 24% of the amount over $85,525
$163,300 - $207,350	$33,271.50 plus 32% of the amount over $163,300
$207,350 - $518,400	$47,367.50 plus 35% of the amount over $207,350
$518,400+	$156,235 plus 37% of the amount over $518,400

---

[1] "Taxable income" refers to the amount that's left after subtracting your deductions from your total income.

Married Filing Jointly (2020)

Taxable income:	The tax is:
$0 - $19,750	10% of the amount over $0
$19,750 - $80,250	$1,975 plus 12% of the amount over $19,750
$80,250 - $171,050	$9,235 plus 22% of the amount over $80,250
$171,050 - $326,600	$29,211 plus 24% of the amount over $171,050
$326,600 - $414,700	$66,543 plus 32% of the amount over $326,600
$414,700 - $622,050	$94,735 plus 35% of the amount over $414,700
$622,050+	$167,307.50 plus 37% of the amount over $622,050

The Self-Employment Tax

In addition to being subject to regular income tax, earnings from a sole proprietorship are subject to the self-employment tax. This tax is calculated (on Schedule SE) by multiplying your net earnings from self-employment by 15.3%.

At first glance, it may seem unfair to subject somebody to an extra tax simply because he or she is self-employed. However, the self-employment tax is really just a substitute for the Social Security and Medicare taxes that are paid on salaries and wages for employees.

For employees, a Social Security tax of 6.2% and Medicare tax of 1.45% are withheld from each paycheck. Then the employer is required to pay a matching amount. As such, the employee is paying 7.65%, and the employer is paying 7.65%, for a grand total of 15.3%. When you run a sole proprietorship, however, there is no employer with whom you can split the bill. As a result, you're stuck paying the entire 15.3%.

There's a maximum amount of earnings that can be subject to Social Security tax each year ($137,700 in 2020). So for earnings above that threshold, the self-employment tax rate is only 2.9% (i.e., just the Medicare tax rate) rather than the whole 15.3%.

Deduction for One-Half of Self-Employment Tax

Because you're paying an additional tax (i.e., the half of Social Security and Medicare taxes that your employer would be paying if you were an employee), Congress decided it would be fair to allow you to claim a deduction for the extra tax paid. As a result, after using Schedule SE to calculate your self-employment tax, you get to claim (on Schedule 1 of Form 1040) an amount equal to one-half of your self-employment tax as a deduction when calculating your adjusted gross income.

Deduction for Pass-Through Income

For tax years 2018-2025, there is a deduction for anybody with "qualified business income," which includes income from pass-through businesses such as sole proprietorships (or partnerships or S-corporations, as we'll discuss in later chapters).

If your taxable income is under a certain threshold, this new deduction is equal to 20% of your qualified business income, but it cannot be greater than 20% of your taxable income excluding net capital gains. The threshold amounts for 2020 are $326,600 if you are married filling jointly or $163,300 if you are single or head of household.[1]

If your taxable income exceeds the applicable threshold, the calculation of the deduction becomes quite a bit more complicated, as three additional limitations come into play. (If your income is in this higher range, it's worth speaking with a tax professional to discuss these limitations and related tax planning opportunities.)[2]

---

[1] For brevity's sake, I am referring to "taxable income" here. More technically, however, we are concerned with "taxable income, before considering the impact of the deduction for qualified business income."

[2] For a more thorough discussion of this deduction, including these limitations, see the following article: obliviousinvestor.com/pass-through-income-deduction/

Chapter 2 Simple Summary

- Sole proprietorships are known as "pass-through" entities because the income from the business is passed through to the owner, showing up on his or her Form 1040.

- The profit or loss from a sole proprietorship is calculated on Schedule C.

- Earnings from a sole proprietorship are subject to the self-employment tax in addition to being subject to regular federal income tax. The self-employment tax is calculated as 15.3% of your net earnings from self-employment (2.9% for earnings above the annual maximum for Social Security tax).

- Schedule SE is used to calculate your self-employment tax.

- For tax years 2018-2025, you can claim a deduction equal to 20% of your "qualified business income" (subject to several limitations). Qualified business income includes income from pass-through businesses such as sole proprietorships.

CHAPTER THREE

Sole Proprietorships: Liability

The primary downside to operating your business as a sole proprietorship is that a sole proprietor is personally liable for all of the debts of the business. This is known as having "unlimited liability."

To elaborate, if anybody has a reason to sue your business, they'll be able to come after your personal assets, not just the money that you have in your business checking account. This means that, if the suit is for enough money, you could end up losing almost all of your personal possessions—your car, your savings, and possibly even your home.

Oh My Goodness That's Scary! (Right?)

For many people, just reading a description of what it means to have unlimited liability is enough to get them searching for information about how to form a corporation. And that's understandable.

But before you go and spend a substantial amount of time and money forming some other type of business entity, spend a little time thinking about how big of a problem unlimited liability really is for *your* business.

For instance, do you offer a service, or do you create and sell a product? In either case, imagine the worst-case scenario, and think about how bad it really is.

Let's say you provide a service. What's the worst thing that could happen if *everything* goes wrong with a client? Does the client lose millions and millions of dollars? Does the client need a trip to the hospital? Or, perhaps, is the worst-case scenario simply that the client is out the money that you charged them?

If you create and/or sell a product, do the same type of analysis. If everything goes as terribly wrong as you could possibly imagine, what happens?

If the worst thing that you can think of isn't really all that bad, then perhaps—despite nearly everything you read online—it isn't necessary to incorporate or form an LLC.

EXAMPLE: A self-employed author who writes and self-publishes science fiction novels probably has much less to worry about regarding liability issues than, say, a restaurant owner.

Chapter 3 Simple Summary

- As a sole proprietor you will have "unlimited liability" for any debts of the business. This means that, in the case of a lawsuit, somebody could come after your personal assets as well as your business assets.

- Depending upon the nature of your business, it's at least possible that unlimited liability isn't that big of a problem.

CHAPTER FOUR

Partnerships: Overview & How to Form Them

As you'll soon see, partnerships are similar to sole proprietorships in many ways, beginning with the manner in which they're formed.

Federal Requirements

Just like a sole proprietorship is automatically formed when one person goes into business, a partnership is automatically formed when two or more people go into business. No official documentation is necessary for a partnership to be formed. As soon as a multiple-owner business begins operating, it's a partnership (unless the owners have already taken actions to incorporate or form an LLC).

While you don't have to file any documents to create a partnership, there is one thing that you'll need to do for the federal government promptly after forming your partnership. You need to get an EIN (Employer Identification Number, a.k.a. "taxpayer ID"). As mentioned previously, obtaining an EIN is fast and free. Just go to irs.gov and search for "EIN application."

Local Requirements

Of course, just like a sole proprietorship, a partnership will likely be required to file some documents at the city level.

Generally speaking, the local requirements (like the requirements for a sole proprietorship) tend to be based upon what type of business you are engaged in rather than what type of legal structure you use for your business. That is, most cities care more about whether you will be providing accounting services, cutting lawns, or opening a restaurant than they do about whether you're a sole proprietorship or a partnership.

If you can't find anything online about the local requirements for forming a partnership, a call to your city clerk's office (or other comparable entity) is likely to give you the information you need.

State and County Requirements

Because partnerships almost always have a name separate from the names of the partners involved, they generally have to make some sort of "doing business as" or "assumed name" filing at the state or county level. Much like the case of forming a sole proprietorship, this filing is often accompanied by a filing fee. And, again, there are several services— one is mentioned in the appendix—that will (for a fee) help you with this filing if you'd rather not deal with it yourself.

Partnership Agreement

Though not required, it's a very good idea to draft some sort of partnership agreement soon after forming a partnership. A partnership agreement is simply a contract between the partners that out-lines exactly how everything will be divided.

At the very least, a partnership agreement should cover:

- How expenses will be divided,
- How profits will be allocated,
- How and when profits will be distributed (as we'll see in Chapter 6, distributions of profit aren't always equal to allocations of profit),

- Which partners will be responsible for which tasks,
- Under what circumstances a partner can sell his or her interest in the partnership to somebody else (if, for instance, one partner has decided she no longer wants to play a role in the business),
- What occurs in the event of death or disability of one of the partners, and
- How major disagreements between partners will be resolved.

Rather than taking the DIY approach here, it is likely to be worth the time and cost to have an attorney craft the partnership agreement, as a professionally crafted agreement will generally do a better job of covering the necessary points.

Chapter 4 Simple Summary

- If the owners don't take any action to incorporate or form an LLC, a multiple-owner business will be a partnership by default.

- Partnerships are required to obtain an Employer Identification Number (EIN). The process is free and can be done easily at irs.gov.

- Many municipalities will require some sort of license to operate a partnership. Generally, the license required depends upon the type of services/products the partnership offers.

- Like a sole proprietorship, a partnership will generally be required to file something along the lines of a DBA at the state or county level.

- It's not required, but a partnership agreement is certainly a good idea to prevent disputes from arising—and to help resolve disputes when they do arise.

CHAPTER FIVE

Partnerships: Taxation

Partnerships themselves are not actually subject to federal income tax. Instead, they—like sole proprietorships—are pass-through entities. While the partnership itself is not taxed on its income, each of the partners will be taxed upon his or her share of the partnership's income.

Form 1065

Form 1065 is the form used to calculate a partnership's profit or loss. On the first page, you list the revenues for the business, list the expenses for the business, and then subtract the total expenses from the total revenues. It's exactly what you would expect.

On the second and third pages of Form 1065 you answer several yes/no questions about the nature of the partnership. For instance, you'll be asked whether any of the partners are not U.S. residents, whether the partnership had control of any financial accounts located outside of the U.S., and other questions of a similar nature.

Schedule K and Schedule K-1

The fourth page of Form 1065 is what's known as Schedule K. Schedule K is used to break down the partnership's income into different categories. For instance, ordinary business income goes on line 1, rental income goes on line 2, interest income shows up a little bit later on line 5, etc.

After filling out Schedule K, you'll fill out a separate Schedule K-1 for each partner. On each partner's Schedule K-1, that partner's share of each of the different types of income is listed.

EXAMPLE: Aaron and Jake own and operate a partnership. Their partnership agreement states that they're each entitled to exactly 50% of the partnership's income. If, on Schedule K, the partnership shows ordinary business income of $50,000 and interest income of $200, each partner's Schedule K-1 will reflect $25,000 of ordinary business income and $100 of interest income. This income will then show up on each partner's regular income tax return (Form 1040).

What's important to note here is that allocations from a partnership maintain their classification when they show up on the partners' individual tax returns. This is important because some types of income are taxed differently than other types of income. For instance, long-term capital gains (gains from the sale of investments that were held for longer than one year) are currently taxed at a maximum tax rate of 23.8%, and in some cases they are not taxed at all.

EXAMPLE: Aaron and Jake's partnership buys shares of a stock, holds the shares for several years, and then sells them for a gain of $10,000. When Aaron's $5,000 share of the gain shows up on his tax return, it still counts as a long-term capital gain (as opposed to counting as ordinary income). It will, therefore, be taxed at a maximum rate of 23.8%, even if Aaron is in a much higher tax bracket.

Similarly, deductions maintain their character when passed through from a partnership. For example, if a partnership makes a cash contribution to a qualified charitable organization, that contribution will maintain its character when it shows up on each of the partners' personal returns. That is, it can be claimed as an itemized deduction, subject to all the normal limitations for charitable contributions (or, for 2020, it can be claimed as an adjustment to gross income of up to $300).

Self-Employment Tax for Partnerships

Ordinary business income from a partnership is generally subject to the self-employment tax when it is passed through to general partners. This makes sense given the rule that we just discussed about income maintaining its classification when allocated to a partner on his or her K-1.

Deduction for Pass-Through Income

Because partnerships, like sole proprietorships, are pass-through businesses, profit from a partnership will also qualify for the deduction for "qualified business income." With a partnership, your deduction is for 20% of *your share* of the partnership's profit, subject to the same limitations mentioned in Chapter 2.[1]

---

[1] Again, the limitations are quite complex. For a more thorough discussion, see this article: obliviousinvestor.com/pass-through-income-deduction/

Chapter 5 Simple Summary

- Like sole proprietorships, partnerships are "pass-through" entities. A partnership is not subject to federal income tax. Rather, its owners are subject to federal income tax on their share of the profit.

- Form 1065 is used to calculate a partnership's profit or loss.

- Schedule K is used to break down a partnership's income and deductions by category. Schedule K-1 is then used to show each partner's allocated share of the various types of income and deductions.

- Income and deductions from a partnership maintain their classification when they are passed through to a partner. For example, long-term capital gains are taxed at a maximum rate of 23.8%, and ordinary business income is subject to self-employment tax.

- For tax years 2018-2025, you can claim a deduction equal to 20% of your share of a partnership's profit (subject to limitations).

CHAPTER SIX

Partnership Taxation (Part 2: Tax Basis)

One thing that surprises the owners of many partnerships when their first tax season rolls around is the fact that partners get taxed on their allocated share of the partnership's profit, even if nothing was distributed to them. The explanation has to do with a concept known as "tax basis."

The general rule is as follows: owners of a partnership are taxed upon their share of the partnership's taxable income, regardless of how much is distributed. A partner is *not*, however, taxed upon distributions he receives from the partnership, so long as those distributions do not exceed the partner's tax basis in the partnership.

What Does "Tax Basis" Mean?

Tax basis refers to the amount of money a person has invested in an asset. A partner's basis in a partnership is:

1) Increased by any amounts he invests in the business,
2) Increased by his share of the partnership's taxable income (and decreased by his share of the partnership's losses),
3) Decreased by the amount of any distributions he receives, and
4) Increased by his share of the debt owed by the partnership.

EXAMPLE: Michelle and Kayla run a partnership and have recently decided to bring on another partner to help with the work. Their friend Tim invests $20,000 and is given a 1/3 ownership interest in the partnership. At this point, Tim's tax basis in the partnership is $20,000.

During Tim's first year in the business, the partnership's taxable income is $90,000. Each partner will be taxed upon his or her share of the taxable income. Tim will be taxed upon $30,000 of income, and his tax basis in the partnership will be increased to $50,000. ($20,000 + $30,000.)

In the following year, the partnership has no taxable income. In March of that year, Tim receives a $35,000 cash distribution from the partnership.

This is not taxable as income. The distribution does, however, decrease his tax basis in the partnership to $15,000. ($50,000 − $35,000.)

In April, Tim receives another distribution, this time in the amount of $20,000. The first $15,000 of the distribution will be nontaxable and will reduce his tax basis to $0. The remaining $5,000 of the distribution, however, *will* be taxable (as a capital gain), because his tax basis cannot be reduced below zero.

Tax Basis for LLC and S-Corp Owners

Like partnerships, S-corporations and multiple-owner LLCs are pass-through entities for federal income tax purposes. (More on these topics in later chapters.) As a result, owners of those businesses—like owners of a partnership—are taxed upon their allocated share of taxable income and are not taxed upon distributions they receive, so long as those distributions do not exceed their tax basis in the business.

Chapter 6 Simple Summary

- In a partnership, the partners are taxed upon their allocated share of the taxable income, regardless of whether or not it is distributed.

- Partners are not taxed upon distributions received from the partnership, so long as those distributions would not reduce their tax basis below zero.

- A partner's tax basis in a partnership is increased by amounts he invests in the partnership, by his share of the partnership's taxable income, and by his share of the debt owed by the partnership.

- A partner's tax basis in a partnership is reduced by distributions received from the partnership and by his share of the partnership's losses.

CHAPTER SEVEN

Partnerships: Liability

It's obvious that before you form a partnership with somebody, you should make sure that he or she is a person you trust and in whom you have confidence. What's not necessarily as obvious is exactly *how much* you must trust this person before forming a partnership actually becomes a good idea.

Unlimited Liability—Even for Each Other!

Generally speaking, every partner in a partnership has unlimited liability for all of the partnership's debts. (Note: limited partnerships, which we'll discuss momentarily, work somewhat differently.) It's very much like a sole proprietor's unlimited liability but with one crucial difference: you're now personally responsible for debts of the business, even if you had nothing to do with creating them.

EXAMPLE: Tom and Jennifer run a local newspaper, and their business is organized as a partnership. One week while Jennifer is on vacation, Tom reprints—without permission—an article from another newspaper. The other paper decides to sue for copyright infringement. Even though Jennifer had nothing to do with the legal infraction, she could potentially be held liable for the entire amount of the judgment. Such is the risk of being a partner in a partnership.

Of course, Jennifer might be successful if she took Tom to court to sue for the amount that she ended up paying. But she'd still be out the cost of the legal fees, not to mention the hassle involved.

Partners as Agents of the Partnership

Each partner can be held responsible not only for liabilities resulting from a lawsuit, but also for liabilities stemming from a contract signed by only one of the partners. This is due to the fact that each partner is an "agent" of the partnership. As an agent, each partner has the legal power to bind the partnership—and thus each of the partners—to a contract.

Fortunately, there are some limitations to a partner's power as an agent of the partnership. Most importantly, each partner can only act as an agent in affairs that are within the scope of the partnership's business. For example, if you run a retail store that sells locally grown produce, you don't have to worry about your partner buying a sailboat under the name of the partnership. Given that the purchase of a sailboat is clearly outside the scope of the business, your partner would have no power as an agent to bind the partnership to the contract.

Limited Partnerships

So far, our discussion of partnerships has been about what are known more precisely as "general partnerships." In addition to general partnerships, there is another form of partnership known as the "limited partnership." Generally speaking though, whenever somebody simply uses the term "partnership," he's referring to a general partnership.

The difference between the two structures is that, in a limited partnership, there are two types of partners: general partners and limited partners. General partners have unlimited liability for the debts of the partnership, while limited partners do not. Limited partners (much like shareholders of a corporation) cannot lose an amount greater than their investment in the partnership. A limited partnership can have as many or as few of each type of partner as it wants, with the notable exception that there must be at least one general partner.

One important rule about limited partnerships is that the limited partners cannot participate in managerial decisions or in the day-to-day operation of the partnership. If they do, they'll lose their limited liability. Therefore, in many limited partnerships, the general partners are the original founders, and the limited partners are outside investors.

Chapter 7 Simple Summary

- In a general partnership (commonly referred to as simply a "partnership"), each partner has unlimited liability for all of the partnership's debts.

- Each partner, as an agent of the partnership, has the power to bind the partnership to a contract.

- Partners do not, however, have the power to bind the partnership to contracts that are clearly outside the scope of the business.

- In a limited partnership, limited partners have limited liability. They can only lose the amount that they have invested. General partners in a limited partnership have unlimited liability.

- Limited partnerships can have as many or as few limited partners as they choose, but they must have at least one general partner.

- Limited partners cannot engage in the management or day-to-day operations of the partnership.

PART TWO

Your Other Options: LLC, C-Corp, or S-Corp

CHAPTER EIGHT

LLCs: Overview & How to Form Them

LLCs are created under state law, not federal law, so the precise rules will vary somewhat from state to state. That said, the general idea behind the creation of the LLC was for it to provide business owners with the best of both worlds:

- The relative simplicity afforded by pass-through tax treatment (discussed in Chapter 9), and
- Liability protection (discussed in Chapter 10), previously only available through incorporation.

Forming an LLC: Articles of Organization

Again, the specifics vary from state to state, but in most states an LLC is formed by filing a document known as your articles of organization with the Secretary of State. Generally, your articles of organization must include:

- Your LLC's name and the address of its principal place of business,
- The names of the owners (referred to as the members) of the LLC,
- The nature of the LLC's business, and
- The name and address of the LLC's registered agent (the party authorized to accept delivery of legal documents—such as notice of a lawsuit—on behalf of the LLC).

Of course, your state may require your articles of organization to include other information in addition to the above.

Qualifying for Business in Other States

If you plan to do business in states other than the one in which your LLC is formed, you may be required to file some sort of documentation with the

Secretary of State in each of those states. This process of filing with other states is known as "qualifying" or "foreign qualifying" your LLC in those states.

Generally, the question of whether or not you'll have to qualify your LLC in a state comes down to whether or not the LLC will have a physical presence in that state. A physical presence is just what it sounds like: an office, retail location, warehouse, etc. Having employees in a state is also likely to make it necessary for your LLC to qualify there. The rules vary from state to state, so be sure to find out what the requirements are for the states with which your business will have any interaction.

Operating Agreement

If your LLC is going to have multiple owners, you should definitely create an operating agreement. An operating agreement does for an LLC what a partnership agreement does for a partnership. It outlines:

- How expenses will be divided,
- How profits will be allocated,
- How and when profits will be distributed,
- Which owners (members) will be responsible for which tasks,

- Under what circumstances a member will be allowed to sell his/her interest in the LLC,
- What occurs in the event of death or disability of one of the members, and
- How disagreements between members will be resolved.

As with the crafting of a partnership agreement, the crafting of an LLC operating agreement is one of those times where it's likely to be worth the cost of hiring an attorney to do the work. An agreement crafted by a non-professional is likely to omit something important.

Transitioning from Sole Proprietorship to LLC

Generally, the move from sole proprietorship to limited liability company isn't terribly complicated. The primary reason for the ease of this transition is the fact that (as we'll see in the next chapter) the transition from sole proprietorship to LLC is a non-taxable event.

EXAMPLE: Kalinda runs a sole proprietorship working as a personal chef. She decides, for liability reasons, to form an LLC. After filing all the appropriate paperwork to establish the LLC, all she has to do is transfer the ownership of the business-related assets (business checking account, equipment, etc.) to the LLC. This transfer of assets is a nontaxable event. That is, it will not have any impact on her federal taxation for the year.

Transitioning from Partnership to LLC

The move from partnership to limited liability company isn't complicated either. The reason is (again) that the transfer of assets is a nontaxable event, provided that the LLC is owned by the same people, in the same proportions, as the original partnership.

EXAMPLE: Eric and Karl are equal partners in an event planning business. Their business is growing, and they decide that it would be wise to form an LLC in order to limit their potential liability should something go wrong with one of their clients. After forming the LLC (with 50/50 ownership, just like the original partnership), they transfer all of the assets that were previously owned by the partnership so that they are now owned by the LLC. This transfer causes neither taxable income nor a deduction for the partnership or its owners.

Do it Yourself, or Get Help from a Pro?

Should you decide to form an LLC, one of the questions you'll have to answer is whether you want to tackle the paperwork on your own or find a professional to take care of it for you. Generally your options break down into three different categories:

1) Hire an attorney,
2) Use an online service (e.g., legalzoom.com), or
3) Do it yourself after researching the steps involved in the process.

Of course, the obvious disadvantage of using an attorney is that it's going to be the most costly option. The tradeoff is that you're going to get somebody who knows your state's laws and who knows your personal situation.

Using an online service will generally cost less than hiring an attorney, and any reputable online service will know the filing requirements for all 50 states. The downside is that you won't get the personalized advice on which entity to choose. In addition, you won't get personalized assistance with crafting an operating agreement between you and any other members of the LLC.

I generally recommend against attempting the process entirely on your own, regardless of how much research you've done online. Many people who take this approach end up forgetting something important. Given the affordability of most of the online services, it doesn't make sense not to get any help—especially when compared with the hassle of having to go back and change something later, or having to prepare some document in a rush because your banker or insurance agent needs to see it. There's even the possibility that, if you really mess up the formation process, your LLC won't legally exist, and you'll think you're protected from personal liability when in reality you are not.

Who is Allowed to Form an LLC?

One final thing to note about forming an LLC is that, depending upon your business, you may not actually be eligible to form one. In some states, anybody can form an LLC. In other states, certain professionals (doctors, for instance) are barred from forming an LLC. In still other states, professionals are allowed to form an LLC, but it must be a "professional limited liability company" (PLLC), which will be subject to additional regulations. So, as always, be sure to check your own state's rules.

Sometimes, states that do not allow the above-mentioned professionals to form an LLC will allow them to form a "limited liability partnership" (LLP). LLPs are taxed the same way as regular partnerships—and thus, the same way as multiple-owner LLCs as we'll soon see.

The potential liabilities for partners in an LLP are the same as for partners in a general partnership, with one major exception: partners are not personally liable for lawsuits that arise from another partner's malpractice. Each partner is, however, still liable for lawsuits arising from his or her own malpractice. (In some states, partners in an LLP also have protection from liabilities resulting from the LLP breaching a contract.)

Does an LLC need an EIN?

If an LLC has multiple owners or has any employees, it will need to obtain an Employer Identification Number. Again though, even if your business isn't required to get an EIN, you may want to do so anyway so as to avoid sending out your Social Security number to clients and vendors.

For single-member LLCs without employees, even if you do obtain an EIN, you should continue to use your Social Security number (rather than the EIN) for federal tax reporting purposes.

Chapter 8 Simple Summary

- The first document you'll have to prepare (in most states) when forming an LLC is your articles of organization.

- If you plan to have a physical presence or employee in any state other than the one in which your LLC is formed, you'll likely be required to file some documentation with that state. This process is known as foreign qualification.

- If your LLC is going to have more than one owner, it's a very good idea to create an operating agreement to prevent disputes from arising in the future and to help settle disputes when they do arise.

- Transferring assets from a sole proprietorship or a partnership to an LLC results in neither taxable income nor a deduction (as long as the LLC is owned by the same people, in the same proportions, as the original business).

- It's generally unwise to attempt the LLC formation process without any assistance.

CHAPTER NINE

LLCs: Taxation

As far as federal income taxes are concerned, LLCs don't really exist. The Internal Revenue Code—the body of law that outlines all federal income taxation—treats each LLC as if it were one of the other types of entities.

Specifically, unless they have elected otherwise, single-member LLCs (LLCs with one owner) will be taxed as sole proprietorships, and multiple-member LLCs will be taxed as partnerships. Because of this tax treatment, LLCs—like sole proprietorships and partnerships—are often referred to as "pass-through" entities.

EXAMPLE: Kali owns and operates a restaurant as a sole proprietorship. She later decides to form an LLC for her business. The business will continue to be taxed as a sole proprietorship (for federal tax purposes at least).

EXAMPLE: Steve and Beth own and operate a winery. After learning about the potential dangers of unlimited liability in a partnership, they decide to form an LLC. The business will continue to be treated as a partnership for federal income tax purposes.

LLCs Taxed as Corporations

Sometimes, after forming an LLC, the owner(s) of the LLC will decide that they would benefit from being taxed as a C-corporation rather than as a sole proprietorship or partnership. (We'll cover C-corp taxation in Chapter 12.) When this happens, the owners have two options:

1) Form a corporation and transfer all of the assets from the LLC to the corporation, or
2) Fill out a form (Form 8832) electing corporate tax treatment for the LLC.

The second option is certainly the easier and less costly of the two.

The same thing can be done should the LLC's owner(s) decide that S-corporation taxation would be beneficial. The only difference is that a different form (Form 2553) is used to notify the IRS of the election.

Disregarded Entities

If a single-member LLC does not elect to be taxed as a corporation, it is referred to as a "disregarded entity" because its existence is disregarded entirely as far as federal income tax is concerned. (That is, the LLC and its owner are considered to be one and the same.)

State Taxation of LLCs

Again, unless an election is made otherwise, LLCs will be treated as either sole proprietorships or partnerships for federal tax purposes. However, depending upon where your business is located, state income taxes might not work the same way.

For example, some states tax LLCs directly on their income rather than (or in addition to) taxing the owners on their share of the income. For instance, in California, LLCs are subject to an $800 annual tax, as well as an income-based annual fee if the LLC earned more than $250,000 in California that year.

EXAMPLE: Braden runs a sole proprietorship in California for his part-time video production business. He earns roughly $3,000 per year from the business and is considering forming an LLC. However, even with an annual income of only $3,000, a

California LLC would still be subject to a tax of $800—or more than one-quarter of the business's total profit. Braden eventually decides that the benefits of forming an LLC would be outweighed by this disproportionately large tax.

Before deciding to form an LLC, it's definitely a good idea to find out precisely how your state taxes limited liability companies.

Chapter 9 Simple Summary

- For federal tax purposes, single-owner LLCs are treated as sole proprietorships, and multiple-owner LLCs are treated as partnerships.

- An LLC can elect to be taxed as a corporation simply by filing a form with the IRS (Form 8832 for C-corporation tax treatment or Form 2553 for S-corporation tax treatment).

- Some states do not tax LLCs the same way that the federal government does, so be sure to find out how your own state taxes LLCs before creating one.

CHAPTER TEN

LLCs: Liability

Generally speaking, the reason for forming an LLC is to obtain some protection from unlimited liability. And part of the reason that LLCs have become so popular in recent years is that they usually do a good job of providing such protection.

That said, the limited liability provided by an LLC is not perfect, so it's essential to be aware of the types of situations in which having an LLC would *not* protect you from personal liability.

Personally Guaranteeing Business Debt

Generally speaking, the owner of an LLC will not be personally liable for satisfying a contract between the LLC and another party. However, at the risk of stating the obvious, if the owner of an LLC *personally* guarantees a loan for the business, the lender will be able to hold the LLC owner personally liable for payment of the debt, regardless of the fact that the business is an LLC.

Of course, the lesson here is to do everything possible to avoid personally guaranteeing a business loan. Unfortunately, if your business is new, it's likely that creditors will be unwilling to loan you a large amount of money unless you are willing to be on the hook for it personally or pay a very high interest rate.

Liability Resulting from Tort of the LLC Owner

The word "tort" refers to wrongful acts (other than breaches of contract) that result in legal liability to somebody. For example, harmful negligence in the performance of a service for a client would be a form of tort. In most cases, the owner of an LLC will not be held personally liable for torts committed by employees of the business. Forming an LLC will *not*, however, protect you from the liability resulting from torts that you personally commit.

EXAMPLE: Karen owns a dental practice, organized as an LLC. In addition to owning the LLC, Karen also performs dental services for patients on the

LLC's behalf. The LLC also employs Kyle to perform similar services.

One day while performing oral surgery on a patient, Karen's attention wanders, and she ends up severely damaging a nerve, causing the patient to permanently lose feeling on one side of his face. The patient will be able to hold both Karen and the LLC liable for the malpractice.

If, however, it had been Kyle's negligence that harmed the patient, the patient would probably not be able to hold Karen personally liable. (He would still, however, be able to hold the LLC liable.)

Professional Liability Insurance

The fact that you are personally liable for your own torts (regardless of whether you have formed an LLC, corporation, etc.) is a primary reason that most business owners should consider purchasing professional liability insurance (referred to as errors and omissions insurance or malpractice insurance in many fields).

Piercing the Corporate/LLC Veil

Whenever you read anything about the limited liability provided by an LLC or corporation, you're likely to encounter the term "piercing the corporate veil." This term refers to the fact that, under certain circumstances, a court may decide that a corporation or LLC is not materially separate from its owners and that the plaintiff should be allowed to come after the owners for their personal assets.

Some of the factors that may lead to a court piercing the LLC veil include:

1) Fraudulent behavior on the part of the LLC or its owners,
2) Intermingling of funds between the accounts of the LLC and the accounts of the owners,
3) Undercapitalization of the LLC (i.e., the LLC was formed without enough funding to be able to satisfy its existing and likely obligations),
4) Absence of financial records (especially records of transactions between the LLC and its owners), and
5) Anything else that would lead a court to believe that the LLC is merely a formality, and is not materially distinct from its owners.

Chapter 10 Simple Summary

- If you end up personally guaranteeing a business loan, you're going to be held personally responsible for its repayment, regardless of the fact that your business is an LLC.

- Even if you form an LLC, you are still liable for your own torts. (This is a major reason why most business owners should consider purchasing professional liability insurance.)

- Important steps toward preventing a court from piercing the LLC veil include: keeping the owners' personal finances and the LLC's finances separate, keeping excellent records (especially for transactions between the LLC and its owners), and providing the LLC with sufficient funding for normal operations.

C-Corporations: Overview & How to Form Them

Corporations are either C-corporations or S-corporations. The only difference between a C-corp and an S-corp is the way in which each is taxed. (We'll discuss this more fully in later chapters.)

When a person uses the word "corporation," she may be referring to either C-corporations or to corporations in general (both C and S). You'll generally be able to figure it out from context without too much difficulty.

How to Form a Corporation

The options for forming a corporation are the same as for forming an LLC:

1) Research the process and do it yourself,
2) Use an online service, or
3) Enlist the aid of an attorney.

What makes the situation different from forming an LLC is the level of complexity. Forming a corporation requires more work, and there are more things that could potentially be messed up. Again, I'd recommend against attempting to do it on your own. I'd suggest using either an online service or a local attorney—preferably the attorney.

Tax Consequences of Forming a C-Corporation

As we'll discuss more fully in the next chapter, C-corporations are separate entities from their owners. As a result, there can be tax consequences when you transfer the business-related assets into the name of the corporation. For example, if the transaction in which you form the corporation involves you contributing services, contributing property subject to a mortgage, or receiving any property other than stock in the newly formed corporation, you may have to recognize income as a result of the transfer.

As you might imagine, it's probably a good idea to get a tax professional's advice on how to do the transfer so you can structure it in the most advantageous way.

Eligibility for Forming a Corporation

In many states, there are certain types of professionals who aren't allowed to form a regular corporation. These professionals must instead form "professional corporations" or "professional service corporations," which are subject to additional regulations. Professionals who are frequently required to form such professional corporations include:

- Accountants,
- Doctors and other healthcare professionals (nurses, pharmacists, psychologists, etc.),
- Engineers,
- Lawyers, and
- Social workers.

This varies from state to state, so it's worth checking with your Secretary of State.

Qualifying for Business in Other States

As with other types of businesses, if your corporation will have a physical presence or employees in a state other than the state in which it is formed, it is important to check with the Secretary of State in that other state to see if you need to go through a "foreign qualification" process.

Chapter 11 Simple Summary

- Corporations can be either C-corporations or S-corporations. The only difference between the two is taxation.

- Forming a corporation is more complicated than forming an LLC, so it's probably a good idea to enlist the help of an attorney as well as a tax professional.

- In many states, certain professionals are required to form a special type of corporation if they want to incorporate.

CHAPTER TWELVE

C-Corporations: Taxation

Corporate taxation is unique in that the business itself is subject to an income tax. Note how this is different from a sole proprietorship or a partnership in which the business itself is not taxed, but the owners are taxed based upon their allocated share of the income.

A C-corporation's income tax is unaffected by how many owners (shareholders) the corporation has or by how much of the profit is distributed to the owners. Prior to 2018, C-corporations were taxed with a progressive rate schedule like individuals (i.e., with lower tax rates at lower levels of income and higher tax rates at higher levels of income). For tax years 2018 and onward, however, C-corporations are taxed at a flat 21% tax rate.

Taxation of Dividends

When a corporation makes a distribution of earnings to its owners, the payment is known as a dividend. Dividend income is taxable to the recipient (though it's usually taxed at a maximum rate of 23.8%, as compared to ordinary income, which is taxed at the rates listed in Chapter 2). In other words, corporate profits—if they are paid out to shareholders—are taxed twice: once at the corporate level and once at the shareholder level.

As a result of these two levels of taxation, C-corporation tax treatment is not usually advantageous when compared to pass-through tax treatment in which the profit is only taxed once.

Paying Yourself a Salary

One way to avoid the double taxation of the corporate structure is to pay the owners a salary—or year-end bonus—that will leave the corporation with exactly zero income. (Salaries paid to employees count as deductions for a corporation, thus reducing the corporation's taxable income.)

Of course, the amount received as salary will still be taxable income to the owners. In fact, when a corporation pays its owners a total amount of salary equal to what profits would have been without the salary, the net result is essentially the same as if the business was simply being taxed as a sole proprietorship or partnership.

EXAMPLE: Debbie owns and runs a pizzeria. Her business is currently a sole proprietorship, but she's attempting to determine if forming a C-corp would be beneficial. Her revenues for the year are projected to be $180,000, and her expenses (not counting any salary she pays herself if she incorporates) are projected to be $110,000.

If Debbie continues to run her business as a sole proprietorship, she'll have $70,000 of earnings from self-employment. (And her income tax and self-employment tax will be computed as normal.)

If Debbie decides to incorporate and pay herself a $70,000 salary, the corporation will have a taxable income of $0. She'll have $70,000 of salary, upon which she'll pay regular income tax. She won't have to pay self-employment tax. But she and the corporation will each be responsible for 7.65% in Social Security and Medicare taxes, totaling 15.3% anyway.

End result: Debbie pays the same total amount of tax in each scenario.

Potential for Savings: Income Splitting

But what if a business owner doesn't need every last dollar of her business's profits in order to pay her personal bills? In some *uncommon* situations, high-earning business owners (those in the 32% tax bracket or above) *might* find C-corporation tax treatment to be a tax-reduction tool if they leave some money in the business's bank account indefinitely (i.e., they do not distribute it as a dividend).

In such a strategy, the owner has the corporation pay her a salary, but not a salary so large that it wipes out the corporation's profits entirely. The end result is that the corporation has some taxable income, and the owner has some taxable income. The tax savings are achieved because:

1) The income is split between the owner and the corporation (thus keeping the owner in a lower tax bracket), and
2) The profit is never distributed (or is distributed at a later time when the owner's income is much lower and she therefore faces a 0% tax rate on dividends), so the "double taxation" never occurs.

Accumulated Earnings Tax

If you're considering the income splitting strategy, you'll want to be sure to steer clear of the accumulated earnings tax. The accumulated earnings tax is a 20% tax imposed on a corporation for earnings that accumulate (i.e., that are not distributed to owners as a dividend) that are in excess of the business's reasonable needs. Accumulations of less than $250,000[1] are generally considered to be within the business's reasonable needs, but to avoid the tax on accumulations in excess of that amount, the corporation must demonstrate a specific, feasible plan for the use of those earnings.

Personal Holding Company Tax

A personal holding company is a corporation that:

1) Is owned (directly or indirectly) more than 50% by 5 or fewer individuals at any time during the last half of the tax year, and
2) Derives at least 60% of its adjusted ordinary gross income from rent, interest, royalties, and dividends from unrelated corporations.

---

[1] $150,000 for service corporations in the fields of health, law, engineering, architecture, accounting, actuarial science, performing arts, or consulting.

Instead of being subject to the standard accumulated earnings tax, personal holding companies (PHCs) are subject to a 20% tax (in addition to normal income tax) imposed on *any* after-tax net income (other than capital gains) that is not distributed to shareholders. The takeaway: if your corporation is a PHC, the income splitting strategy goes right out the window.

Deduction for Pass-Through Income

Because C-corporations are not pass-through entities, income from a C-corporation does not qualify for the deduction for qualified business income.

Corporate Losses

Just like a corporation's taxable income is not passed through to the shareholders, a corporate loss is not passed through to the shareholders either. In other words, when a C-corporation incurs a loss for the year, that loss cannot be used to offset the owners' other taxable income. Instead, when a C-corporation incurs a loss, the corporation can use that loss as a deduction against its taxable income in future years. (For C-corporation losses arising in 2018-2020, the loss can be "carried back" to offset the corporation's taxable income in the five prior years via an amended return.)

In contrast, operating losses from pass-through entities *can* (with some limitations) be used to offset the owners' other taxable income. Therefore, if you expect to incur losses during the initial years of your business, it may be to your advantage *not* to form a corporation right at the outset.

EXAMPLE: Maria opens a neighborhood bakery. Her business has a slow start, and she incurs a net loss of $15,000 in her first year of operation.

If her business is taxed as a sole proprietorship, Maria will likely be able to use the loss to offset some of the taxable income from her husband's job. If, however, her business is taxed as a C-corporation, Maria will not gain any immediate tax benefit from the loss. Instead, she will have to wait and use the loss to offset the corporation's income in future years.

Form 1120

Form 1120 is the form used for a C-corporation's annual tax return. The first page is where most of the action happens. This is where the corporation's different types of income and deductions are listed.

The second page (Schedule C) is only applicable if the corporation owns shares in other businesses.

The third page (Schedule J) is where you apply any applicable credits and estimated tax payments for the purpose of calculating the amount of the corporation's refund or the amount of tax still owed.

The fourth page (Schedule K) is simply a variety of other questions to be answered—the number and nature of the corporation's shareholders, whether the corporation filed the necessary Forms 1099 for payments it made, and so on.

The final page includes Schedule L (Balance Sheet per Books), Schedule M-1 (Reconciliation of Income/Loss per Books with Income/Loss per Return), and Schedule M-2 (Analysis of Unappropriated Retained Earnings per Books). However, these schedules are not required to be filled out until the corporation has either:

- Assets of $250,000 or more at the end of the year, or
- Total receipts of $250,000 or more for the year.

Chapter 12 Simple Summary

- Unlike sole proprietorships or partnerships, C-corporations are taxable entities. That is, they have to pay tax on the income they earn.

- After a corporation is taxed on its income, it can distribute it to the owners (in a payment known as a dividend). The owners are then taxed on the dividend income, thus resulting in two levels of taxation. Because of these two levels of taxation, C-corporation taxation is not usually advantageous.

- If you are a high-income business owner and your business generates more income than you need for personal use, C-corporation taxation might offer some tax savings via an income splitting strategy.

- When a C-corporation incurs a loss, it cannot be used to offset the owners' other taxable income. The corporation can, however, use the loss to offset its taxable income in the future.

CHAPTER THIRTEEN

Corporations: Liability

For most legal purposes, corporations are distinct entities. In other words, corporations are treated (more or less) as if they were people. They're allowed to own things, rent things, sue or be sued, and so on.

Limited Liability

The reasoning behind the concept of the corporation—a business legally distinct from its owners—was to allow the owners to not have to worry about being held personally liable for the debts of the business. Generally speaking, because the corporation is a separate entity, anybody wishing to bring a lawsuit against the business has to bring it against the corporation rather than against the owners personally.

This protection is in fact one of the fundamental elements of our entire economy. As an example, what are the odds that anybody would have invested in Chipotle or McDonald's if they knew that they could be held personally liable if anybody were to bring a lawsuit against the company as a result of getting sick from one of their products? And who would have bought shares of General Motors if there was a chance they'd be held personally liable for accidents caused by faulty manufacturing?

If corporations didn't offer the protection they do, hardly anybody would invest in new companies.

Planning on Outside Investment? Plan on Incorporating.

For the above-mentioned reason, if you're planning on securing cash from outside investors, it's quite likely that your only option is going to be to form a corporation. (To be more specific, it'll likely have to be a C-corporation due to S-corporation ownership restrictions, which we'll discuss in Chapter 14.)

Another reason that investors are more likely to invest in a corporation is that shares in a corporation can usually be sold more easily than ownership interests in any other type of business. Investors like knowing that if they want to get out, they can.

Ongoing Legal Requirements

One slight drawback to forming a corporation is that there are a few ongoing legal requirements that will take up your time. For example, whenever the directors of a corporation make a major decision, it must be recorded in a document known as a "resolution." A resolution doesn't have to be anything fancy or complicated. Just be aware that forming a corporation means you're going to be in for a little more paperwork. Also, most states require an annual meeting of the directors and shareholders, as well as a record of what was discussed at the meeting. Of course, if you're the only owner, this just means preparing one more document every year, as the "meeting" with yourself probably doesn't have to be very long.

Tort of Corporate Shareholders

As with an LLC, it's possible for the owners of a corporation to be liable as a result of torts they personally commit (e.g., negligence, fraud, etc.), even if the tort was performed in the service of the corporation.

Piercing the Corporate Veil

As with an LLC, in the case of a lawsuit, a court may decide that a corporation is not materially separate from its owners and that the plaintiff should be allowed to come after the owners' personal assets. Factors that could lead to such a decision are similar to those with an LLC, including:

1) Fraudulent activity by the corporation or its owners,
2) Intermingling of funds between corporate accounts and personal accounts of the owners,
3) Disregard for corporate formalities (such as the preparation of resolutions and holding of annual shareholder meetings),
4) Undercapitalization of the corporation (i.e., the corporation was formed without enough funding to be able to satisfy its existing and likely obligations),
5) Absence of corporate financial records, and
6) Anything else that would lead a court to believe that the corporation is merely a formality, and is not materially distinct from its owners.

Chapter 13 Simple Summary

- Generally speaking, the owners of a corporation will not be held personally liable in the case of a lawsuit against the corporation.

- If you plan on attracting many outside investors, you may have to form a C-corporation.

- It's possible for shareholders of a corporation to be held personally liable for torts they commit in the service of the corporation.

- If a court decides that a corporation is not in fact distinct from its owners, the court may decide to "pierce the corporate veil," thereby allowing a plaintiff to come after the involved shareholders' personal assets.

- Important steps toward preventing a court from piercing the corporate veil include: keeping your personal and corporate finances separate, keeping excellent records, following corporate formalities, and providing the corporation with sufficient funding.

CHAPTER FOURTEEN

S-Corporations: Overview & How to Form Them

S-corporations are simply C-corporations that have elected to receive a special kind of tax treatment.[1] In other words, the only difference between an S-corporation and a C-corporation is taxation.

Electing S-Corp Taxation

Electing S-corp taxation couldn't be any easier. All you have to do is fill out a single form (Form 2553),

---

[1] S-corporations get their name from Subchapter S of Chapter 1 of Subtitle A of the Internal Revenue Code, which is where the rules regarding S-corporations can be found.

and your corporation will be taxed as an S-corp for as long as you continue to meet the various shareholder requirements for S-corp taxation (discussed next).

Also, as mentioned briefly earlier, LLCs are allowed to elect S-corp taxation by filing Form 2553.

Who Can Elect S-Corp Taxation?

In order for a corporation (or LLC) to be eligible for S-corp taxation, it must meet all of the following requirements:

1) It must be a domestic corporation or LLC (as opposed to a foreign one).
2) It must have no more than 100 shareholders/members.
3) The shareholders can only be individuals, estates, and tax-exempt organizations. (In other words, no corporations or partnerships as shareholders.)
4) It can have no nonresident alien shareholders.
5) It can have only one class of stock.
6) It cannot be a bank or insurance company.
7) All shareholders must consent to the election.

Effective Date of S-Corp Election

When you elect S-corporation taxation (by filing Form 2553), the election takes effect on January 1 of the following year, with a few exceptions:

- If you file Form 2553 by March 15 of a given year, you can choose to have the election be effective as of January 1 of that year.
- In the year your business is formed, if you file Form 2553 within the first two months and fifteen days of the business's existence, you can choose to have the election be effective for the business's first year.

In some circumstances, the IRS may grant "relief for a late election." That is, they may allow your S-corp election to be effective for a given year, even if you did not file Form 2553 within the first two months and fifteen days of that year. In order to qualify for such relief:

- The business must have been otherwise eligible for S-corp taxation,
- The business must file Form 2553 along with its Form 1120S (the form for an S-corporation's annual tax return),
- The corporation (as well as its shareholders) must not have already reported income for

> the year inconsistently with the S-corp election, and
> * The business must have "reasonable cause" for its failure to file the election on time.

Obviously the term "reasonable cause" leaves a lot of room for interpretation. The IRS tends to grant a good deal of leeway here, but your best bet is certainly to file within the first two months and fifteen days of the year if you want to be sure your election will be effective that year.

Losing S-Corp Status

If at any time your corporation or LLC no longer meets all of the requirements for S-corp taxation, your S-corp election will be terminated automatically. Alternatively, your S-corp election can be terminated by choice at any time, as long as shareholders/members owning more than 50% of the shares of the business consent to the revocation.

If your S-corporation status is terminated, you will have to wait five years before making another S-corporation election, unless you get specific consent from the IRS to do so earlier.

When an S-corp election is terminated, the business will go back to being taxed how it was taxed before the election. That is, a corporation will go back to being taxed as a C-corp, a single-member

LLC will go back to being taxed as a sole proprietorship (unless the LLC had elected C-corp taxation before it elected S-corp taxation), and a multiple-member LLC will go back to being taxed as a partnership (unless the LLC had elected C-corp taxation before it elected S-corp taxation).[1]

---

[1] Businesses that operate as C-corporations prior to electing S-corp taxation would do well to seek counsel from a tax professional, as doing so brings up an assortment of complications. For example, if the business has accumulated (i.e., undistributed) earnings from its years as a C-corp, it must keep its passive investment income (e.g., royalties, rents, dividends, and interest) below 25% of its gross receipts each year, otherwise it can be subject to additional taxes—and possibly even a forced revocation of its S-corp status. See the instructions to Form 1120S for more information: irs.gov/pub/irs-pdf/i1120s.pdf

Chapter 14 Simple Summary

- The only difference between an S-corp and a C-corp is the way in which they are taxed.

- To elect S-corp taxation for a corporation or an LLC, simply file Form 2553.

- In order to be eligible for S-corp taxation, a corporation or LLC must meet several requirements regarding the nature of the business and the number and type of shareholders.

- In order for your S-corp election to be effective for a given year, you should file Form 2553 by March 15 of that year.

- Your business's S-corporation status will be automatically terminated if, at any point, it ceases to meet any of the requirements to be an S-corporation.

CHAPTER FIFTEEN

S-Corporations: Taxation

S-corporations, like partnerships, are pass-through entities. That is, there is no federal income tax levied at the corporate level. Instead, an S-corporation's profit is allocated to its shareholder(s) and taxed at the shareholder level.

Tax Forms for S-Corporations

Form 1120S is the form used for an S-corporation's annual tax return. (This makes sense, given that Form 1120 is used for a regular corporation's annual return.) As with a partnership, Schedules K and K-1 are used to show how the business's different types of income and deductions are allocated among the owners.

No Self-Employment Tax!

The big benefit of S-corp taxation is that S-corporation shareholders do not have to pay self-employment tax on their share of the business's profits.

The big catch is that before there can be any profits, each owner who also works as an employee must be paid a "reasonable" amount of compensation (e.g., salary). This salary will of course be subject to Social Security and Medicare taxes to be paid half by the employee and half by the corporation. As a result, the savings from paying no self-employment tax on the profits only kick in once the S-corp is earning enough that there are still profits to be paid out after paying the mandatory "reasonable compensation."

EXAMPLE: Larissa is the sole owner of her S-corporation, an advertising agency. Her revenues from the business are $60,000 per year, and her annual expenses (not counting salary) total $10,000. Therefore, her S-corp's profit for the year (before subtracting her own salary) is $50,000.

Larissa's plan is to pay herself $40,000 in salary, and count the remaining $10,000 as profit, thus saving money as a result of not having to pay self-employment tax on the $10,000 profit.

Unfortunately, Larissa learns that the average advertising professional in her area and with her level of experience earns roughly $70,000 annually. As such, she's going to have a difficult time making the case that $40,000 is a reasonable level of compensation.

In the end, Larissa ends up setting her salary at $50,000 in order to avoid trouble with the IRS. Sadly, her S-corp's profit (after paying her salary) ends up being $0, so she isn't really saving any money on taxes as a result of S-corp taxation.

Determining a Reasonable Salary

So what's a reasonable salary? This exact question is frequently a topic of debate in court cases between the IRS and business owners who are, allegedly, paying themselves an unreasonably small salary in order to save on self-employment taxes.

What makes the situation tricky is that the tax code itself does not provide any specific guidelines for what's reasonable. That said, the following factors are frequently considered by courts when ruling on the issue:

- The duties and responsibilities of the shareholder-employee,
- The training and experience of the shareholder-employee,
- The amount of time and effort devoted to the business,

- The amount of dividends paid to shareholders (especially as compared to compensation paid to shareholder-employees),
- The wages of the business's other employees (i.e., those who are not shareholders), and
- What comparable businesses pay for similar services.

Cost Basis in an S-Corporation

Much like owners of a partnership, shareholders of an S-corporation are taxed on their *allocated* share of the business's profits—no matter whether or not those profits were actually distributed to them. But, also like an owner of a partnership, a shareholder of an S-corporation is not taxed on distributions from the business, so long as those distributions do not exceed his cost basis in the S-corp.

A shareholder's cost basis in an S-corporation is increased by his allocated share of the business's income and by contributions he makes to the business. His basis will be decreased by his share of the business's losses and by distributions he receives from the business.

EXAMPLE: Austin forms an S-corporation and contributes $40,000 cash to the business. In the calendar year in which the business is formed, the business pays Austin a salary of $30,000, after which it has remaining ordinary business income of $20,000. During the year, the corporation also makes a distribution to Austin of $25,000.

When Austin forms the corporation, his cost basis in the business is $40,000 (the amount he contributed). The $20,000 ordinary business income increases his basis to $60,000, and the $25,000 distribution reduces his basis to $35,000. $35,000 is his cost basis at the end of the first year.

The $30,000 salary will be taxable to Austin as ordinary income, and it will be subject to normal payroll taxes as well. The $20,000 ordinary business income will be taxable to Austin as ordinary income, but it will not be subject to payroll taxes or self-employment tax. The $25,000 distribution will not be taxable to Austin at all, because his cost basis before the distribution was greater than $25,000.

Deduction for Pass-Through Income

Because S-corporations are pass-through entities, profit from an S-corporation qualifies for the same deduction for qualified business income that we discussed in Chapters 2 and 5. That is, you may qualify for a deduction of up to 20% of your share of the S-corporation's profit. Of note, any compensation (e.g., wages/salary) that the S-corporation pays to you is *not* considered to be qualified business income. It is only allocations of *profit* from the S-corporation that are considered to be qualified business income.

State Taxation of S-Corporations

Of course, each state has its own rules regarding S-corp taxation. Some work like the federal income tax in which shareholders pay taxes on their share of the income. Other states tax the S-corp directly. For instance, in Illinois, S-corporations pay a 1.5% tax on the S-corp's Illinois income. This tax is in addition to the income tax that shareholders pay on their share of the S-corp's income.

Chapter 15 Simple Summary

- S-corporations are pass-through entities. That is, the corporation itself is not subject to federal income tax. Instead, the shareholders are taxed upon their allocated share of the income.

- Shareholders do not have to pay self-employment tax on their share of an S-corp's profits. However, before there can be any profits, owners that work as employees for the S-corp will need to receive a "reasonable" amount of compensation.

- S-corporation taxation is similar to partnership taxation in that owners are taxed upon their share of the business's income, regardless of whether or not it is actually distributed to them. Also similarly, distributions from the business are not taxable so long as they are not in excess of the shareholder's basis in the S-corporation.

- For tax years 2018-2025, you can claim a deduction equal to 20% of your share of an S-corporation's profit (subject to limitations).

CHAPTER SIXTEEN

Assorted Drawbacks of Corporate Taxation

While corporate taxation (most often, S-corp taxation) allows for tax savings in many cases, it's important to be aware that it comes with a handful of drawbacks as well, some more significant than others.

Unemployment Insurance Tax

One major ramification of forming a corporation or electing S-corp or C-corp taxation for your LLC is that, assuming you do work for your business, you'll have to become an employee of the business. (This is in contrast to a sole proprietorship or partnership, where the owners are not technically employees.)

As a business with employees, you'll have to register as an employer in your state in order to pay unemployment insurance tax on the salary that the business pays you. The revenue from this tax is what's used to provide unemployment benefits to the unemployed.

This tax obviously cuts into any savings that you might achieve by electing corporate taxation. To see exactly how much it cuts into those savings though, you'll have to do a little research, as the tax rate varies from state to state, as does the applicable "wage base"—the maximum amount of wages per employee upon which the tax is based.

EXAMPLE: Derek is the sole owner of an LLC in Oregon. His profit from the business (before considering any taxes or salary he'd pay himself if the business were taxed as a corporation) is $60,000. Given Derek's line of work, the lowest amount he believes he could pay himself as salary without it being considered unreasonable is $40,000. In Oregon, the unemployment insurance tax wage base for 2020 is $42,100, and the tax rate is 2.1% for all new employers.

If Derek's LLC is taxed as a sole proprietorship, the $60,000 profit will be subject to self-employment tax. If Derek elects S-corporation tax treatment for his LLC and pays himself a $40,000 salary, he'll save $2,358 as a result of not having to pay self-employment tax on the $20,000 after-salary profit.[1] However, he'll have to pay a 2.1% unemployment insurance tax on his $40,000 salary (for a total of $840) that he would not have to pay as a sole proprietor.

The federal government has an unemployment tax too, but the calculation of the tax involves a credit for unemployment taxes paid at the state level. As a result of this credit, the amount you actually owe will usually be quite small (as low as $42 per employee per year).

Employer Filing Requirements

In addition to having to pay unemployment insurance tax on your salary, there are reporting requirements that come with having employees. At the federal level, you'll need to file:

- Form 940 annually to report the Federal Unemployment Tax Act (FUTA) tax for wages you paid,

---

[1] $2,358 is the difference between the $8,478 of self-employment tax that would be owed on a profit of $60,000 and the $6,120 of total payroll taxes that would be owed on a salary of $40,000.

- Form 941 quarterly to report Social Security taxes, Medicare taxes, and withheld income taxes on wages you paid, and
- Form W-2 annually to report wages paid, taxes withheld, and other related information.

You'll also be responsible for making monthly payments of the employer's share of Social Security and Medicare taxes on the wages you paid, plus the amount that was withheld for the employee's share of those taxes as well as income tax. In addition, you'll have to meet annual, quarterly, and possibly monthly filing requirements for your state regarding wages paid and the related taxes.

The takeaway here: if you elect corporate tax treatment for your business, unless you enjoy dealing with paperwork all year long, it's probably wise to find an accountant or payroll service provider to handle these things for you.

Tax Preparation Costs

Not surprisingly, many small business owners choose to outsource their annual tax preparation. One factor that affects the cost of tax preparation is the type of business entity that you've chosen. Tax prep for a sole proprietorship is the easiest (and thus cheapest), followed by partnerships, then S-corporations and C-corporations.

A 2018 survey done by the National Society of Accountants provides us with a little bit of hard data.[1] According to the survey, the average rates for tax preparation were as follows:

Form 1040 Schedule C (Sole Proprietorship)	$187
Form 1065 (Partnership)	$670
Form 1120S (S-Corporation)	$807
Form 1120 (C-Corporation)	$851

These rates include only federal returns. They don't separately state the average cost of tax preparation for an LLC because LLCs are taxed as one of the four types of businesses above.

Reduced Maximum Contributions to Retirement Plans

One additional drawback of corporate taxation is that it often reduces the amount you can contribute to a business retirement plan. For example, as a sole

---

[1] A summary of the survey is available at: mainstreetpractitioner.org/feature/nsas-2018-2019-income-and-fee-survey-is-here/

proprietor, the most you can contribute to a SEP IRA for 2020 is the lesser of $57,000 or 25% of your net earnings from self employment (which works out to be the same as 20% of your business's profit, after subtracting an adjustment for one-half of your self-employment tax and before considering any retirement plan contributions).

But if your business is taxed as a corporation, you will be treated as an employee. And the most that can be contributed to an employee's SEP IRA for 2020 is the lesser of $57,000 or 25% of his/her compensation (e.g., salary).

EXAMPLE: Sandy has an LLC taxed as a sole proprietorship. Prior to considering any retirement plan contributions for the year, Sandy's net earnings from self-employment were $80,000. The most Sandy could contribute to a SEP IRA would be $16,000 (20% of $80,000).

If Sandy had elected S-corporation tax treatment for her LLC and paid herself a $50,000 salary, the most she'd be able to contribute to a SEP IRA would be $12,500 (25% of $50,000).

Reduced Social Security Benefits

In addition to reducing the amount you can contribute to business retirement plans, corporate taxation often reduces the amount of Social Security retirement benefits that you will eventually be able to receive.

When you claim your Social Security retirement benefit, your monthly check is based on your 35 highest years of (wage-inflation-adjusted) earnings—the higher your earnings record, the larger your retirement benefit. If you're a sole proprietor, the entire profit from the business each year (minus the deduction for one-half of self-employment tax, and up to the maximum amount subject to Social Security tax) is what goes into the calculation. In contrast, if you elect S-corp or C-corp taxation, only the amount you pay yourself as compensation (i.e., wages, salary, or bonus) will be included in your earnings record.

Chapter 16 Simple Summary

- If you perform work for your business and your business is a corporation (or an LLC electing S-corp or C-corp taxation) you will count as an employee of the business.

- As an employer, your business will have to pay unemployment insurance tax on salary or wages paid to you.

- As an employer, your business will be responsible for meeting numerous filing requirements throughout the year and for making timely payments to the federal government and to your state government for taxes related to the salary paid to you.

- Tax preparation fees for a business taxed as a corporation are typically significantly higher than those for a sole proprietorship.

- Electing C-corp or S-corp taxation often results in a reduction of the maximum contribution you can make to a business retirement plan as well as a reduction of your Social Security retirement benefit.

CONCLUSION

Putting It All Together

There are two primary reasons that a business owner might want to change from operating as a sole proprietorship or partnership to a different form of business:

1) To save on taxes, and
2) To limit potential liability from the business.

Saving on Taxes

In the absence of an election to be taxed as an S-corp or C-corp, a single-member LLC will be taxed the same way as a sole proprietorship, and a multiple-member LLC will be taxed as a partnership. As a result, simply forming an LLC isn't going to save a person any money on taxes.

Forming a C-corp (or electing C-corp taxation for an LLC) can in some uncommon cases reduce a high-earning business owner's total tax bill. In most cases, however, C-corp taxation is going to *increase* a business owner's total tax bill because of the two levels of taxation (i.e., taxation of the corporation's profit, plus taxation of dividends paid to shareholders). Also, income from a C-corp does not qualify for the deduction for qualified business income (because C-corporations are not pass-through entities), whereas profit from a sole proprietorship, partnership, or S-corporation can qualify.

Forming an S-corporation (or electing S-corp taxation for an LLC) can sometimes result in tax savings, because profits from S-corporations are not subject to self-employment tax. However, before you can achieve any savings as a result of tax-advantaged profit distributions, you'll have to pay each of the employee-shareholders a "reasonable" amount of compensation. Any such wages or salary will be subject to Social Security and Medicare taxes, which will total the same percentage as the self-employment tax anyway. You will, therefore, only save any money if your revenues are sufficiently high for there to be some profit remaining after paying the required salaries.

One major ramification of both C-corp and S-corp taxation is that they result in you becoming an employee of the business. As an employer, your business will be subject to numerous reporting requirements, and it will have to pay unemployment insurance tax on the salary it pays to you. In addition, the amount you can contribute to a retirement plan for your business will likely be reduced, as will the amount of earnings that goes into the calculation of your Social Security retirement benefit.

One final drawback of corporate taxation (both S-corp and C-corp) is that the cost of professional tax preparation services for a corporation is typically significantly greater than the cost of tax prep services for a sole proprietorship (or, to a lesser extent, for a partnership).

Limiting Potential Liabilities

When it comes to limiting a business owner's potential liabilities from the business, just about anything is better than a sole proprietorship (or better than a partnership if it's a business with multiple owners).

Forming an LLC or corporation goes a long way toward limiting the liabilities of the owner(s), but the protection they offer is still not perfect. For example, having an LLC or corporation will not protect business owners from liabilities that result from their own torts. (And this is why most business owners should consider purchasing professional liability insurance.) Nor will having an LLC or corporation protect a business owner from being held liable for a business loan that she personally guaranteed.

In some cases, a court may decide that a corporation or LLC is not, in essence, an entity distinct from its owners and that, as such, a plaintiff should be allowed to come after the business's owners for their personal assets. Such a decision is referred to as "piercing the corporate/LLC veil." The best things a business's owners can do to prevent a court from making such a decision are to keep the finances of the business separate from the finances of the owners, keep excellent financial records for the business, and maintain any corporate formalities that are prescribed by state law.

A Final Thought

If you're still not certain which entity is the best for you, it's probably a good idea to discuss the issue with an attorney and/or tax professional. Also, remember that in some cases it can be reasonable to remain a sole proprietorship (or partnership) for now and revisit the decision as circumstances change.

APPENDIX

Helpful Resources

www.irs.gov
>   The IRS's website. Many articles on IRS.gov are actually written in quite accessible language.

www.ObliviousInvestor.com
>   The author's blog. Includes several hundred articles, covering a wide variety of investing and tax-related topics.

www.legalzoom.com
>   This site can help you with filing a DBA for a sole proprietorship or with forming an LLC or corporation.

IRS Publications

Publication 334 – Tax guide for small businesses

Publication 535 – Business expenses

Publication 463 – Travel, entertainment, gift, and car expenses

Publication 587 – Business use of your home

Publication 946 – How to depreciate property

Publication 541 – Partnership taxation

Publication 542 – Corporate taxation

Publication 505 – Tax withholding and estimated tax

About the Author

Mike Piper is the author of several personal finance books as well as the popular blog ObliviousInvestor.com. He is a Missouri licensed CPA. Mike's writing has been featured in many places, including *Money, The Wall Street Journal, MarketWatch, Forbes,* and *Morningstar.*

LLC vs. S-Corp vs. C-Corp
Explained in 100 Pages or Less

<u>Also by Mike Piper</u>

Accounting Made Simple: Accounting Explained in 100 Pages or Less

Can I Retire? How to Manage Your Retirement Savings, Explained in 100 Pages or Less

Cost Accounting Made Simple: Cost Accounting Explained in 100 Pages or Less

Independent Contractor, Sole Proprietor, and LLC Taxes Explained in 100 Pages or Less

Investing Made Simple: Investing in Index Funds Explained in 100 Pages or Less

Microeconomics Made Simple: Basic Microeconomic Principles Explained in 100 Pages or Less

Social Security Made Simple: Social Security Retirement Benefits Explained in 100 Pages or Less

Taxes Made Simple: Income Taxes Explained in 100 Pages or Less

INDEX

Made in the USA
Monee, IL
29 April 2021

67207686R00069